SPEED!
TRAINS

Jenifer Corr Morse

BLACKBIRCH PRESS, INC.
WOODBRIDGE, CONNECTICUT

To My Godmother, Julie Labrie
–JCM

Published by Blackbirch Press, Inc.
260 Amity Road
Woodbridge, CT 06525
Web site: www.blackbirch.com
e-mail: staff@blackbirch.com

Printed in Belgium

10 9 8 7 6 5 4 3 2 1

Photo Credits
Cover (top left and right, and bottom right), title page, 6-7, 11, 18-19, 21: Corel Corporation; cover (bottom left), page
4: ©Marty Katz/Time, Inc.; pages 8-9: courtesy ALSTOM; pages 12-13: Eurostar international high speed passenger
trains (copyright Eurostar Group Limited; pages 14-15: ©Soile Laaksonen/VR-Group Ltd.; page 17: From the Collections
of Henry Ford Museum & Greenfield Village; page 22: ©Colin Garratt; Milepost 92*/CORBIS.

Library of Congress Cataloging-in-Publication Data
Morse, Jenifer Corr.
     Trains / by Jenifer Morse
     p. cm. — (Speed!)
Includes index.
     ISBN 1-56711-469-5 (alk. paper)
     1. Railroads—Trains—Juvenile literature. [1. Railroads—Trains.] I. Title. II. Speed! (Woodbridge, Conn.)

TF148 .M65 2000
385—dc21   00-011945

Contents

X2000

This high-tech train tilts into curves as it speeds along at 125 miles (201 km) per hour.

This high-speed train from Sweden has reached a top speed of 172 miles (277 km) per hour. By law, however, it is limited to traveling 125 miles (201 km) per hour when it carries passengers. It can accelerate from 0 to 125 miles (200 km) per hour in 3.8 minutes.

The X2000 is capable of reaching a top speed of 172 miles (277 km) per hour.

The X2000 is a tilting train. This means all of the cars except the power unit are able to lean into curves, similar to a motorcycle rider. This lets the train speed through the curves without slowing down. The

tilt helps to balance the train so the riders don't feel seasick. In fact, they hardly notice the 6.5° tilt at all. And the best part about speeding through curvy track is that the train ride is much shorter. Since the X2000 was introduced in 1990, the journey between Stockholm and Gothenburg has gotten an hour shorter!

There are several pieces of advanced technology that help the X2000 function. The Automatic Train Control (ATC) can gather information about the track 2.5 miles (4 km) ahead and relay it to the driver. And an accelerometer in the front car can measure the acceleration on the curves and send a message to the other cars so they will tilt at just the right angle.

Nozomi

This "bullet" train is the fastest passenger train in the world.

The Japanese 500 series Nozomi is the fastest passenger train in the world. It travels at an average of 162 miles (261.8 km) per hour between the Hiroshima and Kokura stations. The 120-mile- (192-km) long journey only takes 44 minutes. The Nozomi also has one of the fastest operating speeds. On a route called the Sanyo Line, this speeding train can travel between Osaka and Hakata at a rate of 186 miles (300 km) per hour. This journey only lasts 2 hours and 17 minutes.

The sleek and powerful Nozomi is both fast and quiet. Its pointed nose is 49 feet (15 m) long and cuts through the air at top speed with little wind resistance. Shock-absorbing dampers are fitted between each car to minimize the vibrations felt inside the train. The usually noisy pantograph—which transfers power currents to the train from overhead wires—is insulated at the bottom. Its supports also have small, wind-cutting projections, which were modeled after the silent flapping of an owl's wings.

The vehicle is made out of aluminum alloy and was developed by the West Japan Railway Company.

The Nozomi can speed along at an average of 162 miles (261.8 km) per hour.

Fast Fact

* Length: 1,325 ft (404 m)
* Height: 12 ft   (3.7 m)
* Width: 11 ft   (3.4 m)

Japan has always led the way for high-speed train service. In 1964, the country's fastest train reached 131 miles (210 km) per hour. The 500 series Nozomi premiered on March, 22, 1997.

AVE

Spain's high-speed answer to Japan's "bullet" train

The Alta Velocidad Espanola, or AVE as it's known, translates into "Spanish high speed" in English. On the high-speed line between Madrid and Seville, the AVE can reach a top speed of 186 miles (300 km) per hour. The 293-mile (471-km) journey lasts 135 minutes—about 30 minutes less than on a regular train. Its best average speed is 130 miles (209 km) per hour.

The AVE is actually a tilting TGV, the same model used in France. Because it can tilt on its track, the train is able to lean into curves without slowing down (also similar to Japan's Nozomi). Ten cars make up the AVE, including two power units, seven passenger cars, and a buffet car. This speedy convoy can carry 325 passengers.

The AVE premiered in April 1992 and was an instant hit. By November of that year, the train had already carried more than 1 million people. Because these trains compete with the airlines for passengers, the AVE was designed to offer everything that is offered on a jumbo jet. Meals are brought to passengers' seats, each traveler can access music stations, and both public and private phone services are available. The AVE also shows onboard movies and television shows.

★ Length: 656 ft   (200 m)
★ Weight: 432 tons

Seville was chosen to test the first high-speed train service in Spain because it was the location of the World Expo in 1992. It is also a popular tourist destination for French visitors.

Spain's AVEs are high-speed tilting trains similar to the Nozomi.

Union Pacific Big Boy

One of the largest and strongest steam engines in history

One of the largest and strongest steam engines ever created, the Union Pacific Big Boy was built for pure power. During the 1930s, the majority of U.S. freight was moved by railroad. In some places, such as the steep mountain areas of the mid-Atlantic states, freight trains had a tough time pulling their loads up and down. Often, two empty trains were used to help pull a freight train up a hill and then to help it descend safely. This practice, however, was very expensive and time-consuming.

To solve their problem, Union Pacific designed a steam engine like no other. The Big Boy weighed 1.2 million pounds (.54 million kg) and produced 6,200 horsepower.

The Big Boy was as powerful as three smaller engines. It was capable of pulling a 3,800-ton freight train with 120 cars through the mountains at a speed of 40 miles (64 km) an hour. Even though it was capable of reaching 80 miles (129 km) per hour, the heavy loads rarely allowed the Big Boy to run at top speed.

Fast Fact

★Length: 132 ft   (40 m)

In its day, the Big Boy carried 28 tons of coal and 24,000 gallons (90,847 l) of water, which it used up in about 3 hours! This giant machine has about a mile of tubes and flues inside its boiler.

Union Pacific's Big Boy produced 6,200 horsepower and could pull 3,800 tons of freight.

The Eurostar connects England and France by traveling through a high-speed tunnel.

Fast Fact

★ Length: 1,292 ft   (393.7 m)
★ Width: 9.2 ft   (2.8 m)

The Eurostar is a very large train. With its 18 passenger cars, it is capable of carrying 794 people. That's about the same number of travelers that can fit on two jumbo jets!

Eurostar

This big train can carry enough passengers to fill two jumbo jets.

The Eurostar is truly an international powerhouse. This high-speed train transports passengers between London, England; Paris, France; and Brussels, Germany. During the trip, the Eurostar is able to run on three different tracks and power systems. Through the French portion of the journey, the Eurostar can reach a top speed of 186 miles (300 km) per hour. The train also connects major European destinations, including the French Alps and Disneyland Paris.

The Eurostar is a popular way to travel between England and France. The trip from London to Paris takes only three hours. The same trip by car, regular train, or ferry would take up to 10 hours. The Eurostar is much faster and more convenient because it doesn't have to slow down for traffic jams or bad weather conditions.

Another reason the Eurostar journey is so quick is the Channel Tunnel (known as the "Chunnel"). It is a 31-mile- (50-km) long underwater train tunnel that connects Calais, France to Dover, England. Nearly 23 miles (37 km) of the Chunnel are 150 feet (46 m) below the water's surface. The Eurostar only takes about 20 minutes to travel the tunnel, driving at a top speed of 100 miles (161 km) an hour.

The Eurostar began service in November 1994 and was the first high-speed train to connect England to the rest of Europe.

Pendolino

Lightweight and electric, this train has super acceleration.

The Pendolino is the fastest train in Finland. It is can reach a top speed of 137 miles (220 km) per hour and can accelerate from 0 to 60 miles (100 km) per hour in just 57 seconds. That's pretty fast, considering that this train weighs about 315 tons! The Pendolino accelerates with 2,700 horsepower, but also has a powerful braking system. The train can come to a complete stop from 88 miles (100 km) an hour in just 2,657 feet (810 m).

Because it is electric, there is no need for a heavy engine to weigh the train down. Its aluminum construction means the train is light. This light weight helps the Pendolino operate at such high speeds.

The Pendolino is a tilting train that is made in Italy. In Italian, the word "pendolino" actually means "pendulum"—a swinging object.

●≡Fast ≡Fact●

* ★ Length: 522 ft (159 m)
* ★ Height: 12 ft   (3.7 m)
* ★ Width: 10 ft   (3.2 m)

Communication on the Pendolino is especially excellent. Not only can passengers use phones, faxes, and overhead projection on board, information monitors in each coach detail the train's progress along the route.

A lightweight, aluminum frame allows the Pendolino to reach high speeds quickly.

2-6-6-6 Allegheny
The largest and most powerful steam engine ever built

The 2-6-6-6 Allegheny locomotive is the largest steam engine in the world. Weighing more than 1.2 million pounds (.54 million kg), the Allegheny was a true powerhouse when it was in use. It was able to produce up to 8,000 horsepower—more than any other steam engine ever.

This steel monster played an important role in moving railroad freight through parts of the United States during the 1940s and 1950s. The Chesapeake & Ohio railroad ran coal trains through the Allegheny Mountains in West Virginia. The 13-mile (21-km) trip included a steep climb to the top of a 2,072-foot-(631.5-m) high mountain, and an equally sharp descent. Few of the steam trains available were up to the job.

The first 10 Alleghenies entered into service in December 1941. With one train pushing and one pulling, these new super machines were capable of moving the coal through the mountains with amazing speed. Even though the Allegheny was designed to run at 45 miles (72.4 km) per hour while pulling 5,000 tons of coal, they were generally used to haul 10,000 tons of coal at 15 miles (24 km) an hour.

Fast Fact

★Length: 126 ft   (38.4 m)

The Virginian railroad was the only other service to use the 2-6-6-6 Allegheny. These trains were called Blue Ridge locomotives and were in service between 1945 and the late 1950s.

The 2-6-6-6 Allegheny produced an amazing 8,000 horsepower.

TGV

One of the fastest trains in the world

The Train a Grande Vitesse—or TGV—is one of the fastest trains in the world, and many countries have modeled their high-speed train service after it. The name TGV refers to the individual trains, the rails they ride on, as well as the entire French high-speed rail system.

The top speed for commercial service on the TGV is 186 miles (300 km) an hour. During special testing conditions, however, the train has reached a speed of 320 miles (515 km) per hour. There may be certain speed restrictions on

●≡Fast ≡Fact●

★ Length: 205.8 ft   (62.7 m)
★ Height: 13 ft   (4 m)

TGV trains vary from 207 feet (63 m) to 1,758 feet (536 m) in length. Most TGV trains are made of steel. Some of the newer trains have aluminum body shells and use magnesium seat frames.

France's TGV trains were the models for many other high-speed services.

some lines or trains, but the weather conditions never affect the speed of the train.

The TGV trains have some design features that set them apart from other high-speed trains. The front and back of each car share an axle, instead of each having its own set of wheels. This axle placement makes the overall train lighter and quieter. Signals are also sent through the train rails so the engineer can read information on the on-board computer. This ensures that the signals posted outside the speeding train are not accidentally misread.

The TGV program began in the late 1960s, when regular railroad tracks were upgraded to accommodate high-speed trains. The TGVs were very popular, and many travelers chose to journey by railroad instead of by airplane. In fact, the TGV was so successful that it paid for itself in less than 10 years.

ICE

Capable of reaching a top speed of 205 miles (330 km) per hour

The ICE—or Inter-City Express—is a high-speed train that operates throughout Germany. The ICE 3, a newer version, debuted in May 2000. It has reached a top speed of 205 miles (330 km) per hour, but averages around 120 miles (193 km) per hour for passenger service.

The main difference between this train and earlier models is that the ICE 3 does not have a power unit. Instead, the power and traction are distributed throughout the entire train. Because the new trains have been designed to operate in several different countries, the cars are shorter and narrower. The ICE 3 is equipped with a signaling system that can also be used in the Netherlands and Switzerland.

The ICE 3 is made up of eight cars with powered axles. In first class, there is a video screen on the back of each seat so the passengers can watch movies as they travel speedily to their destination.

Newer model ICE trains are designed to speed through various countries in Europe.

★ Length: 656 ft (200 m)
★ Width: 10 ft (2.9 m)

The fastest average speed for the ICE is 125 miles (200 km) per hour between the towns of Fulda and Wuzburg. This means Germany has the 5th fastest train service in the world.

401 071-6

Inter-city 225

This passenger train goes forward and backward without changing engines.

The Inter-city 225 is the fastest train running in the United Kingdom. Its name refers to its top speed of 225 kilometers, or 140 miles, per hour. The Inter-city 225 runs on the East Coast Mainline. The track is about 400 miles (644 km) long and connects London, England and Edinburgh, Scotland. The entire journey takes about four hours.

The Inter-city 225 consists of a class 91 locomotive that pulls 9 passenger cars and 1 driving van trailer (DVT). The DVT, located at

The Inter-city 225 is the UK's fastest passenger train.

the back of the train, makes the Inter-city 225 different from other high speed trains, which have an engine on both ends. When a route is completed, most trains with only one engine usually wait for the locomotive to be detached from the front and brought

around to the back, so the train can return in the opposite direction. On the Inter-city 225, however, the engineer can simply walk to the other end of the train and control the vehicle from the DVT. Instead of pulling the train on the reverse trip, the locomotive actually pushes it!

The engine that is able to both push and pull this 476-ton train produces more than 6,000 horsepower! The Inter-city 225 can normally seat just over 500 passengers.

Glossary

accelerate: to go faster and faster

axle: a rod in the center of a wheel, around which the wheel turns

horsepower: a unit for measuring the power of an engine

pantograph: an instrument on the roof of a train that receives the electricity from the overhead wires

traction: the gripping power that keeps a moving object from slipping on a surface

For More Information

Books

Coiley, John. *Eyewitness: Train.* New York, NY: Dorling Kindersley Publishing, Inc., 2000.

Morris, Neil. *Trains.* Englewood Cliffs, NJ: Silver Burdett Press, 1997.

Weitzman, David L. *Locomotive: Building an Eight-Wheeler.* Boston, MA: Houghton Mifflin Company, 1999.

Web Site

National Railway Museum

See photos of and learn more about historic trains—**www.nrm.org.uk**

Index